Critical Thinking Skills

FOR SELECTIVE SCHOOL TESTS, OPPORTUNITY CLASS TESTS AND PROBLEM SOLVING

BOOK 1

Mohan Dhall

Five Senses Education Pty Ltd
2/195 Prospect Highway
Seven Hills 2147
New South Wales
Australia

First Published 2021

Dhall, Mohan
Critical Thinking Skills – Book 1

ISBN 978-1-76032-379-0

Contents

Foreword

Critical thinking is an essential skill that students need to develop. Critical thinking is evidenced when students can analyse data, evaluate options and alternatives and critique information for its coherence. It also is evidenced when students ask meaningful questions, can hypothesise, and also explain reasons to account for observed relationships and patterns. Students who can generalise from the specific and can then appraise their generalisations, and who can propose and justify solutions to complex problems, all demonstrate critical thinking skills.

In a rapidly changing world, characterised by multiple and competing information sources, developing critical thinking skills and the ability to reason logically has never been more important. Critical thinking is a fundamental skill for a meaningful life.

Practice on the problems in this book will help students to develop a range of critical thinking skills. Prior to practising, students should read through the section at the start which provides strategies. Using these strategies will be helpful to developing the skills required to think through complex problems.

The author would like to acknowledge Michael McKay who assisted with editing, made helpful suggestions and whose graphic work can be seen in Questions 14, 16 and 27, and in the fully worked solution for Question 19.

About the author

Mohan Dhall is an experienced teacher and teacher-educator, author and educational manager. Trained in gifted education, Mohan has developed many critical thinking courses for students and has also trained teachers in critical and creative thinking skills. As Director, he ran one of Australia's longest running school based centres for gifted children. He has written hundreds of different types of critical thinking questions and had more than 70 books published. Mohan is currently the Academic Leader of M2K Education and Advisory.

Critical Thinking - An Introduction

Critical thinking involves the application and the development of a number of different thinking skills. Aspects of critical thinking include skills involving each of the following:

- Analysing
- Interpreting
- Evaluating
- Explaining
- Justifying
- Sequencing
- Reasoning – deductive and inductive
- Comparing
- Questioning
- Critiquing
- Inferring
- Hypothesising
- Appraising
- Assessing
- Testing
- Generalising
- Extrapolating and interpolating

At the core of many of these thinking skills is logic. Logic is an application of the principles of reasoning to evidence or data. Two important aspects of logical reasoning are deductive reasoning and inductive reasoning.

Deductive reasoning
This type of thinking requires a person to be able to draw valid or certain conclusions from a premise or premises as well as the application of defined rules.

Inductive reasoning
This type of thinking requires a person to be able to draw general conclusions from the premises which may not be certain. The generalisation should be plausible, but there will not be certainty.

Students may find that they are distracted by generalisations that are plausible but are not assured.

Strategies for dealing with arguments

Critical thinking can be demonstrated by the way a student analyses an argument. In order to analyse an argument, students must firstly clarify what it is that is being argued. Once this has been done, they need to remove distractors based on one or more of the following:

- Relevance
- Hearsay
- Opinion

Relevance Rule
Here something may be written that acts as a distractor. It tests the person's power to discern between what is important and what is not. If the statement or sentence is not relevant, then it should be ignored. Only information that is relevant – or appropriate to the argument – should be included in reasoning. Non-relevant or irrelevant information needs to be put aside.

Hearsay Rule

Here a statement is made that is second hand or from a third party. It may take the following form, "I heard Jake say that he saw what happened". It is information that is not from a person who has direct experience, but rather conveyed through another person. The value of this as evidence to support an argument is **discarded** as it is not reliable.

Hearsay cannot be substantiated or verified and consequently can be untrue or inaccurate and misleading. It can also take the form of gossip or exaggeration.

Opinion Rule

A person's opinion does not add strength to an argument as their opinion is subjective. The aim is to support or understand an argument on the basis of objective evidence supporting the data or hypothesis.

Expert opinion – the exception to the Opinion Rule

The exception to the opinion rule is that of an expert opinion. An expert is someone who will have a view based on evidence and scientific understanding or weight of experience. A professional who gives an informed opinion may be able to give an expert opinion that is important to recognise.

Example

Donald: "If all people who speed are given a fine that is matched to their income then the effect will be fairer. Why should rich people pay the same fine as poorer people? If a poor person pays a $200 fine then this has a huge impact on their weekly income, but it has no effect on a rich person. So, a rich person should pay $15,000 or $20,000 or more, depending on their income. In this way the punishment will have the same effect on both people instead of poorer people being unfairly penalised."

Sussan: "But a $200 fine for each person who commits the same offence is equality and that is fair. No nation in the world could have the system you suggest.

Donald: "In Switzerland they have the system of fining people according to their income."

Sussan: "This is just trying to make all people the same so that there are no rich people, and everyone is the same."

Donald: According to the recently published report by Dr Bradley from the Centre of Crime Statistics, this change would have a positive effect on offending rates.

Sussan: I was speaking to a judge and she said that Dr Bradley was wrong.

What is the **assumption** that Sussan makes in her second response?

A That everything she states is true

B That rich people should have different rules to others

C That all rich people speed when driving

D That poor people deserve to be poor

Donald's argument: everything he says needs to support this premise

Example

Donald: "**If all people who speed are given a fine that is matched to their income then the effect will be fairer**. Why should rich people pay the same fine as poorer people? If a poor person pays a $200 fine then this has a huge impact on their weekly income, but it has no effect on a rich person. So, a rich person should pay $15,000 or $20,000 or more, depending on their income. In this way the punishment will have the same effect on both people instead of poorer people being unfairly penalised."

Sussan: "But a $200 fine for each person who commits the same offence is equality and that is fair. **No other nation in the world could have the system you suggest**."

A reference to other nations is irrelevant

Donald: "**In Switzerland they have the system** of fining people according to their income"

Reference to evidence to counter Sussan's statement. This now makes Sussan's statement relevant as Donald has leveraged it to support his argument

Sussan: "**This is just trying to make all people the same** so that there are no rich people and everyone is the same."

Logical fallacy based on inductive reasoning. An incorrect generalisation has been made here. It also implies a certain opinion: 'all rich people speed.'

Donald: According to the **recently published report by Dr Bradley from the Centre of Crime Statistics**, this change would have a positive effect on offending rates.

Evidence to support the argument. The evidence comes from a known authority and would constitute either factual (objective) support or expert opinion.

Sussan: I was speaking to a judge and **she said that** Dr Bradley was wrong.

Opinion

A That everything she states is true

B That rich people should have different rules to others

C That all rich people speed when driving

D That poor people deserve to be poor

We can identify this assumption as when Sussan says "there would be no rich people" she is implying that all rich people would be subject to higher fines based on income and therefore, by implication, all rich people speed.

Using Venn Diagrams to organise data

Sometimes, the use of Venn Diagrams can assist with solving problems. Consider this question: How can the relationship between men, fathers, widowers and brothers be represented?

Answer

Let Men = M, Fathers = F, Widowers = W and Brothers = B

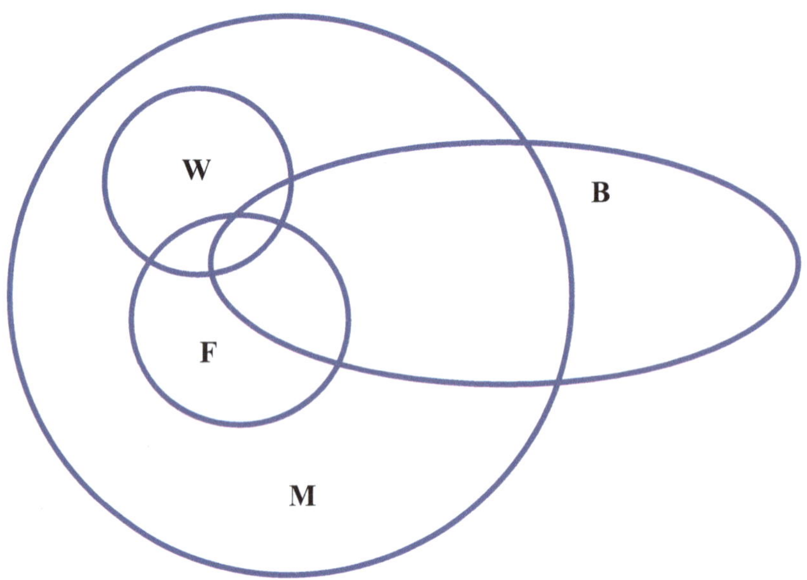

So, how do the shapes relate to the data

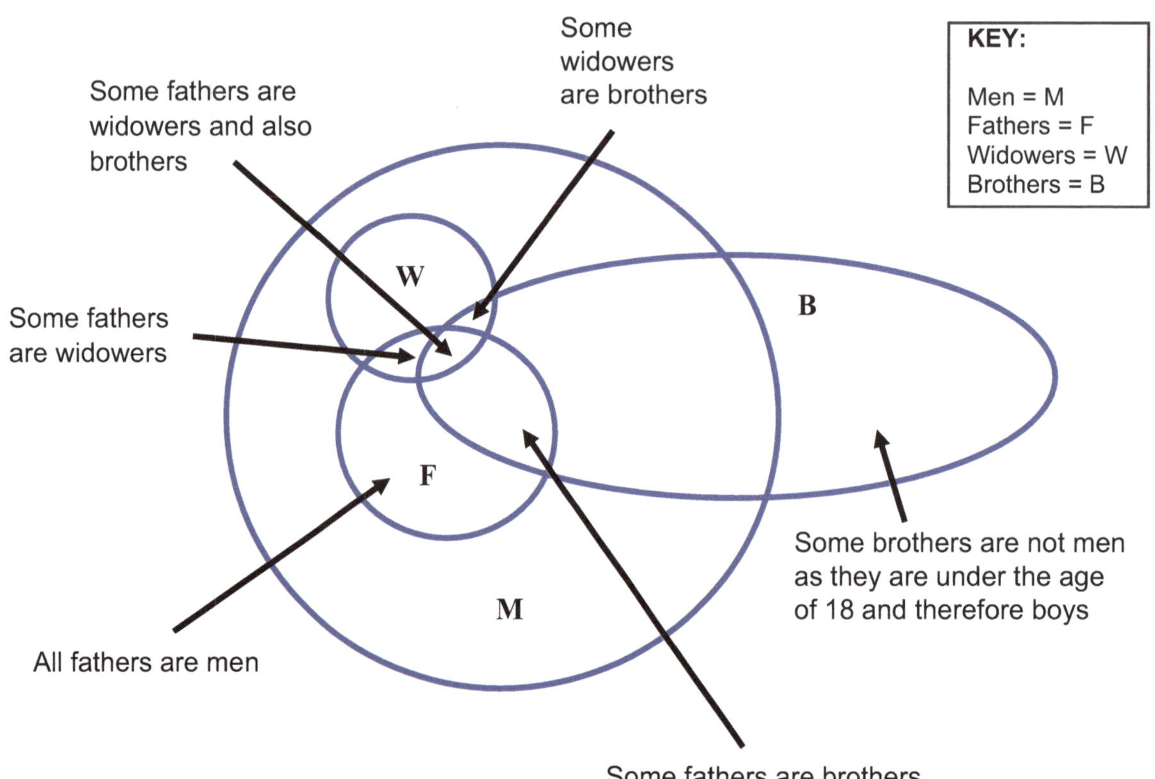

General strategies for dealing with different questions

When presented with information, rules and data, it is important to keep a clear mind about what the problem requires and what information, facts and relationships have been given. A strategy for dealing with complicated information is to write down, in shortened notation, what has been given.

Other strategies include:

1. Reading ALL of the information provided before answering the question.
2. If there is information given in bullet points, then number the bullet points. When applying the information, a reference can be made to the numbered point. This will ensure that the data is being used and applied. This has been demonstrated in the answer section.
3. Read ALL of the answers before making a selection.
4. Even if you think the answer is A or B, complete reading ALL of the answers prior to making your selection.
5. Use diagrams as a means of interpreting and arranging information, particularly relationships between information points. Thus, if you have to arrange people, runners, cars or different items on the basis of a colour, characteristic or value then be sure to 'place' the item to assist with ordering.
6. Be prepared to keep more than one piece of information in your mind at a time. You will need to do this when there are different rules given to information.
7. DO NOT use your general knowledge to answer any of the questions. All the information you need is in the question. No extraneous information should be required to successfully answer the questions.
8. Identify the type of question being asked so that you know what thinking skills you will be utilising.
9. If there is visual stimulus, look at it carefully and try to determine the relationships between the relevant parts of the stimulus.

Critical Thinking Problems

Question 1

Mai, Fred and Alexa have 50 cards each. They take it in turns to roll a dice.

- If the number rolled is odd, then that player has to give the number of cards shown on the face of the dice to each of the other two players.
- If the number rolled is even, then that player receives twice the number of cards shown on the face of the dice from each of the other two players.

Mai rolls a 5.

Fred rolls a 2.

If the friends end up with 28, 55 and 67 cards respectively, which number does Alexa roll?

A 1

B 2

C 3

D 4

Question 2

When Ben told Davo that he was thinking of giving up playing sport to focus on becoming a pilot, Davo said, "You don't need to give up playing sport just because you want to be a pilot. It's good for you to train and play. Playing sports helps keep you fit and strong so that you can also study with clarity."

Which one of these statements, if true, most **strengthens** Davo's argument?

A To play sport well a person needs to practise often.

B Ben's parents think sport is a waste of his time.

C Fine motor skills are needed when flying an aeroplane.

D Ben's neighbour is a pilot who plays soccer.

Question 3

“Whoever fixed the fan must have had both a ladder and a screwdriver”.

If this is true, then which of these statements is also true?

A If Jessie has a ladder and a screwdriver, she fixed the fan.

B If Martha did not have a ladder, she could not have fixed the fan.

C If Hester did not fix the fan, she cannot have a screwdriver.

D If Hester did not fix the fan, she does not have a ladder.

Question 4

A bald man and a man with long hair are discussing tea. The bald man states, “I love Chai Latte”. The long-haired man states, “I love Dandelion tea”. It is known that one of the men loves Chai Latte and one loves Dandelion tea. At least one of the men is lying.

Which of the following is correct?

A The bald man is telling the truth.

B The long-haired man cannot be lying.

C Both of the men are lying.

D The long-haired man does not love Chai Latte.

Question 5

A digital display consists of seven segments which light up in different combinations to produce digits. For example, to display the digit '1' the two right-hand segments normally light up as shown:

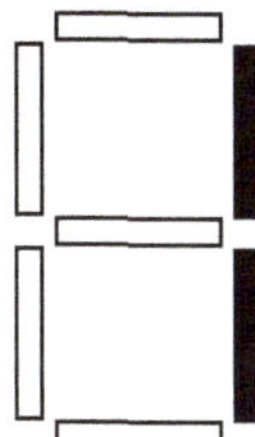

The display is used to show, in sequence, each of the digits 0 to 9. However, the display is faulty and **two of the segments** are not working. Two of the digits in the sequence are displayed as follows:

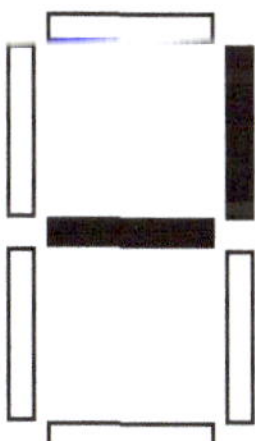

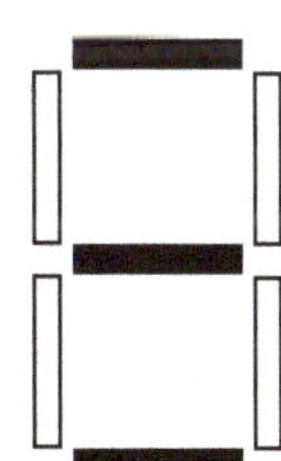

What is the next number in the sequence, as shown by the faulty display?

A

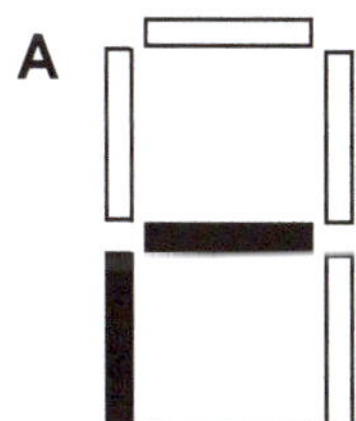

B

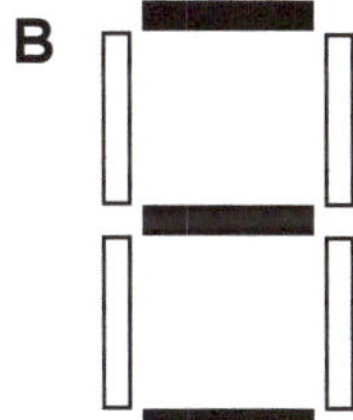

C

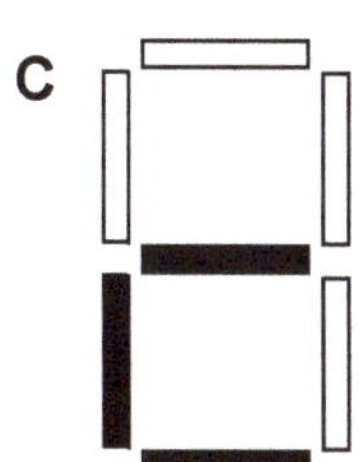

D

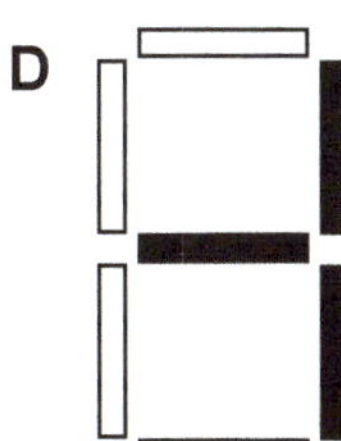

Question 6

Under the best conditions Albert will drive to or from work in 15 minutes.

- If it is raining it takes Albert longer to drive to work than if it is sunny or cloudy.
- If Albert starts his drive to work between 8 AM – 9 AM or drives home from work between 5 PM – 6.30 PM it takes longer.

Today, Albert took 16 minutes to get to work and it was not sunny.

Based on the information provided what is the correct conclusion that can be drawn?

A It must have been rainy.

B Albert left home late.

C Albert drove to work between 8 AM – 9 AM.

D It was either rainy or Albert drove to work between 8 AM – 9 AM.

Question 7

The children Ravi, Dwight, Han, Leo, Vuong and Aaron are all friends and were all born in the same year. Han was born two months before Dwight. Vuong and Leo were born in the same month. Ravi is 5 months younger than Han. Leo was born in August. Aaron is younger than Dwight and older than one other person and was not born in the same month as anyone else.

Only one of the following is true. Which is it?

A Ravi was born in October.

B Dwight was born in May.

C Aaron was born in July.

D Aaron was born before Vuong.

Question 8

A farmer has 264 female ostriches.

This year all but 10 of them have had chicks. One has three chicks and all the rest have either one or two chicks. 360 chicks have been born in total.

How many of the ostriches have had exactly one chick?

A 149

B 104

C 253

D 53

Question 9

Jason bought a bike on the 29th day after January finished and rode it straight away.

Which of the following could not necessarily be true?

A The bicycle was bought in February but used first in March.

B Two weeks after the bicycle was bought, it was March 14th.

C The bicycle was bought in February.

D The bicycle will first be used in March.

Question 10

Pritipath says that electrical cars are better for the environment than petrol cars. However, without enough places to recharge, they are not reliable. In addition, they can only be driven 200 km before needing to recharge. The cars are being used more and more around the world and some governments even have them in their fleets.

Which one of these statements, if true, most **strengthens** Pritipath's argument?

A Many Australian cities and towns are far apart.

B One in every twenty-five petrol stations have charging ports.

C Electric car batteries are very heavy and slow vehicles down.

D Electric cars are more expensive than regular vehicles.

Question 11

In a 2-kilometre running race, prizes are given out to the runners who finish first, second and third in two age divisions: under 16-years and 17–25-years. Prizes are also given to anyone who can run faster than 3 minutes 30 seconds per kilometre.

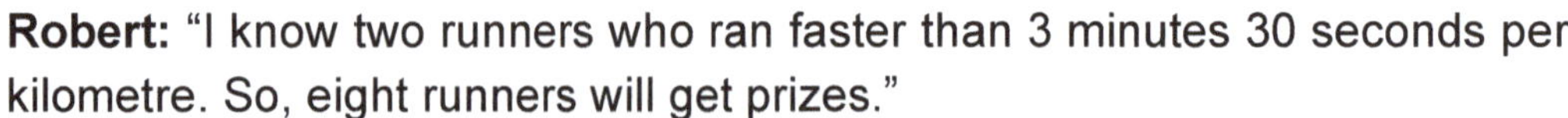

Robert: "I know two runners who ran faster than 3 minutes 30 seconds per kilometre. So, eight runners will get prizes."

Which one of the following sentences shows the **mistake** Robert has made?

A Some runners might run faster than 3 minutes 30 seconds for one of the two kilometres.

B Many runners might find it difficult to run faster than 3 minutes 30 seconds per kilometre.

C We do not know the total number of runners in the race or in each age group.

D The running times may have been by runners who finished first, second, or third.

Question 12

To become a successful pilot, you need to be mathematically brilliant, have perfect sight and also be able to effectively multitask.

Davis: "Serena is very logical and mathematically strong – she loves working out complex mathematics in her head – and always manages several things at a time. She's certain to become a brilliant pilot."

Amira: "Lomu enjoys mathematics but sometimes forgets basic number rules. However, he does have the ability to do many things at a time. I do not think he can be a pilot."

Josie: "Because Roshni wears glasses, she will need contact lenses if she is to be a pilot."

If the information in the box is true, whose **reasoning** is correct?

A None of them

B Amira only

C Josie only

D Davis only

Question 13

There are six people sitting in a row on seats waiting to see a doctor. The seats are numbered 1–6 from left to right. There are three women and three men. They are called Mark, Katy, Vesna, Steve, David and Wendy.

- The men sit on the odd numbered seats.
- Each person owns and drives a car.
- Three cars are black, one is silver, one is red and one is blue.
- Katy drives a black car.
- Mark is four seats to the left of David.
- One of the women has a red car and one of the men has a blue car.
- David's car is not black or blue.
- The women sit in reverse alphabetical order.
- One person beside Mark drives a red car.

Who is sitting in Seat 4 and what colour car does the person have?

A Vesna who drives a black car.

B Vesna who drives a silver car.

C Katy who drives a black car.

D Vesna who drives a red car.

Question 14

The following shapes are used to make a square. However, one piece is missing.

Which of the following pieces completes the square?

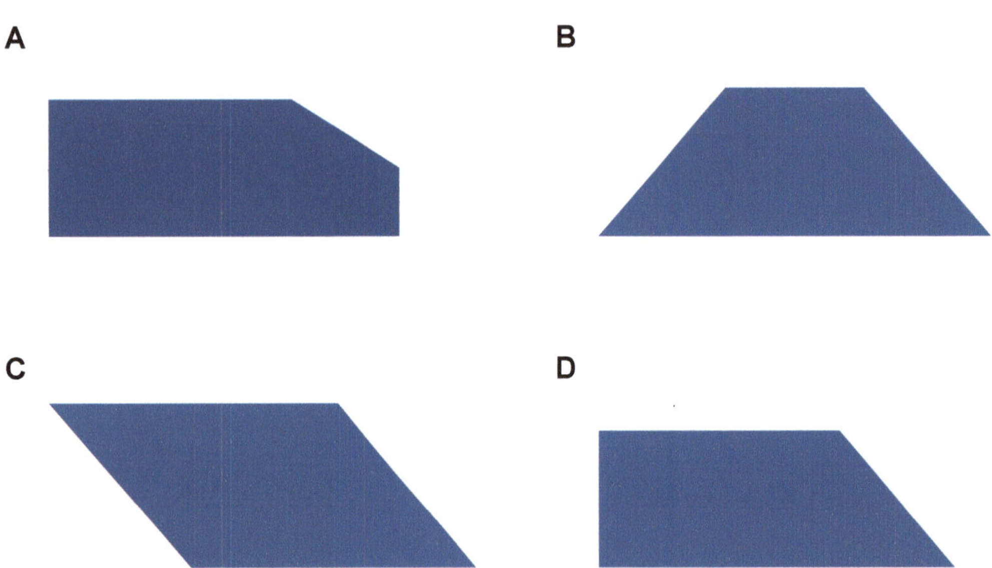

Question 15

There are 14 students in the class studying Business. They each take three tests. The first two are marked out of 50 and the final is marked out of 100. The results of the first two tests are shown below.

Name	Test 1 Mark	Test 2 Mark
Nancy	38	43
Ratnayke	47	38
Zoe	35	34
Warren	41	40
Khuong	27	34
Lam	40	38
Andrew	28	29
Lilith	33	33
Nicholas	39	40
Peter	31	27
Cindy	37	36
Justyn	42	41
Jacqueline	29	33
Alira	49	47

A prize is awarded to the student with the highest combined total score from the three tests. If two students are tied for the highest score, nobody gets the prize.

As the scores stand after two completed tests, one student is able to be sure to win this prize as long as a high enough score is achieved in the final test.

What is the minimum score in the final test that will guarantee this student is awarded the prize?

A 88

B 89

C 90

D 91

Question 16

On the floor of a bathroom is the following set of tiles. Each square tile is identical. Some damage has occurred to the pattern and the grey square shows the part that needs to be replaced.

Which of the following represents the correct pattern to properly complete the patterns?

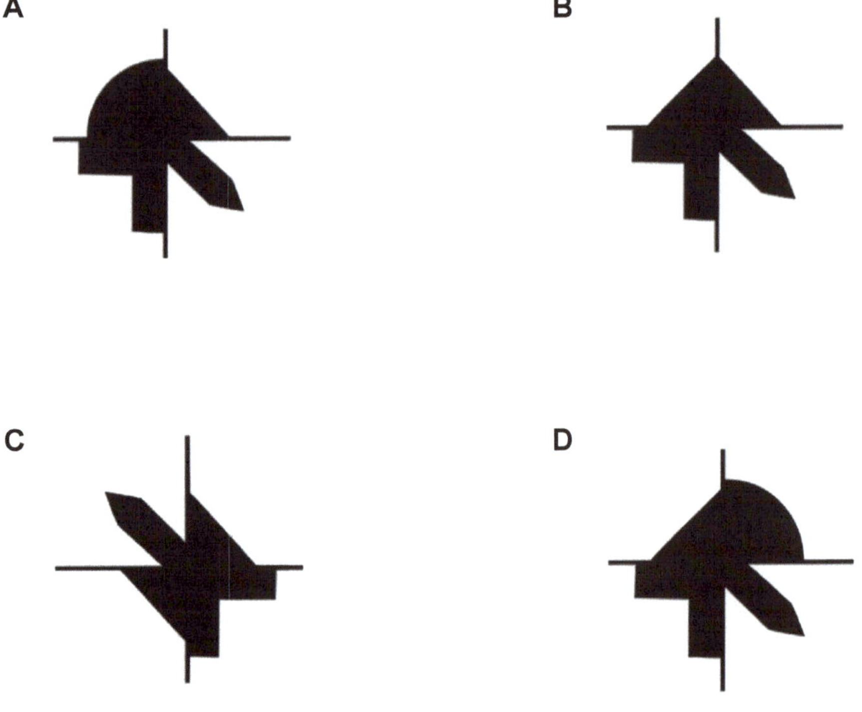

Question 17

There are five people in a car race: Stephanie, Simon, Anna, Emily and Leon. You know the following:

- Simon's car, which is not green or red, finished ahead of three others.
- Emily, in a black car, was behind Anna.
- There are two cars between Stephanie and Anna.
- The green car came first.
- When Leon finished in his silver car there were four cars ahead of him.
- The black car finished 3rd.

Which of the following is true?

A Leon won the race in his silver car.

B Emily finished third in a black car.

C Stephanie came third in a red car.

D Anna's green car was ahead of Simon's red car.

Question 18

Understanding fire and fire behaviour is important. When the fuel load in forests is high, the fire danger is also high and fires can burn rapidly. If there has been drought, the fire danger rises. Out-of-season hazard reduction burning in bushland helps to reduce the probability of intense fire. Over time, fires have become more intense and harder to manage.

Wind speed is also a factor affecting fires. High wind speed can lead to spot fires and also increase flame intensity.

Which of the following if true, **strengthens** the argument above?

A There were more fires this year than last year.

B Firefighters are better trained and have better equipment than they used to have.

C The oils in native trees can make fires behave in unusual and dangerous ways.

D Firefighters in other nations agree that domestic fires are unusually intense.

Question 19

Nadia is standing on the X and facing North.

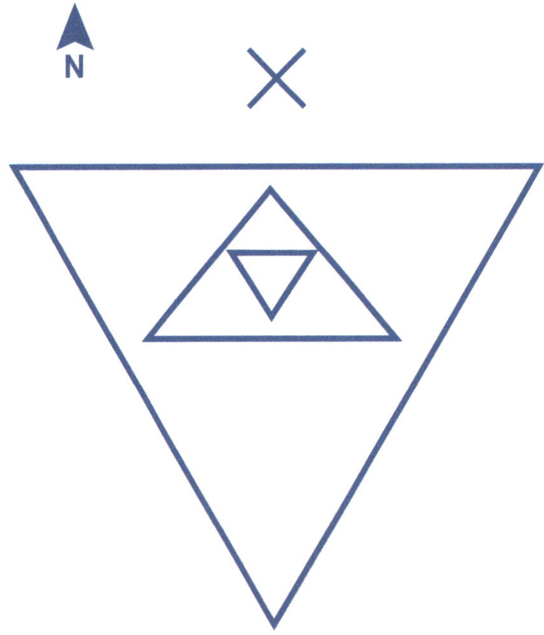

If she faces South, what can Nadia see?

A

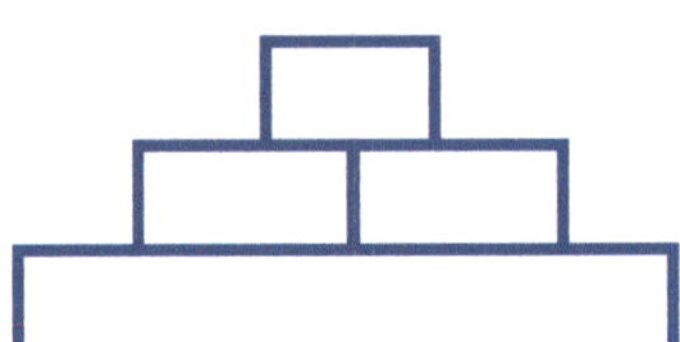

B

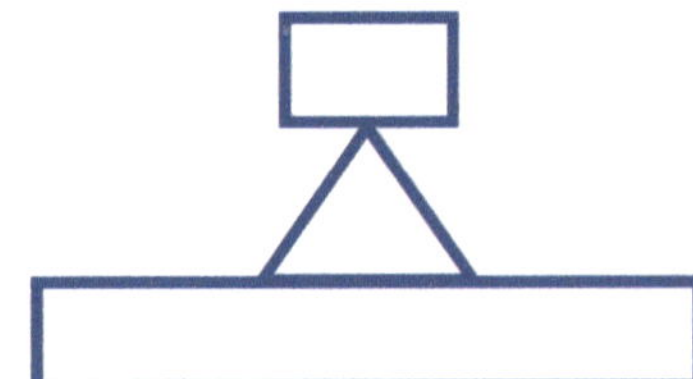

C

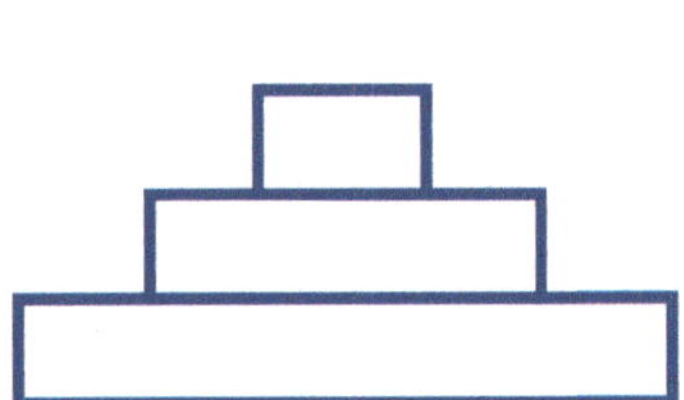

D

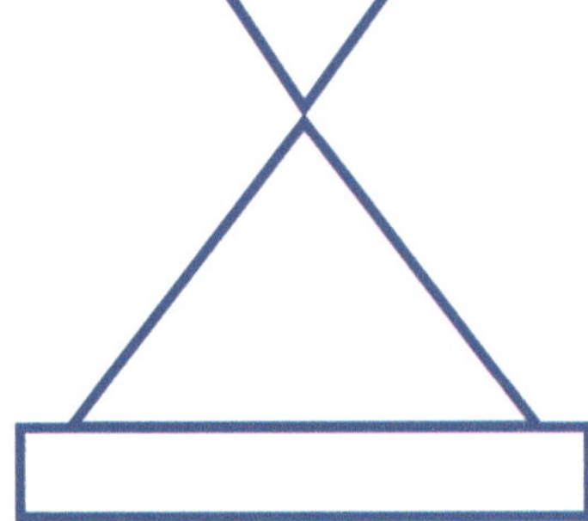

Question 20

The seahorse is a Hippocampus and is the only fish where the male bears the unborn young.

Ngoc: "If you see a male fish bearing young it must be a seahorse."

Stacy: "Also, if you see a fish bearing young, and you know it is not a seahorse, then it cannot be a male."

If the information in the box is true, whose reasoning is correct?

A Neither Ngoc or Stacy

B Ngoc only

C Stacy only

D Both Ngoc and Stacy

Question 21

The prices for cinema tickets are listed below.

Single movie: $12

Three movies in a month: $20

3-month movie pass – can watch 4 movies in each month: $50

What is the lowest amount Donna can pay to watch 14 movies in the next 2 months?

A $100

B $90

C $82

D $94

Question 22

A cricket ball will swing if any one or more of the following apply:

- It is bowled faster than 130 km per hour.
- One side of the ball is smooth, and the other side is rough.
- The ball is held with the seam on an angle.

Jacob: "That ball swung so it must have had one smooth side."

Ashlee: "The seam was vertical, so it must have been bowled at over 130 km per hour."

Which of the following sentences shows the **mistake** that Ashlee has made?

A Ashlee does not know how fast the ball was bowled.

B The ball may have had a rough side.

C The ball may have been angled.

D Other factors such as humidity can make a ball swing.

Question 23

An object that changes its speed or its direction will have accelerated.

Wilma: "If I swing my hand in a circle my finger will be accelerating."

Tuan: "If I stop walking, I will have accelerated."

If the statement in the box is true, whose **reasoning** is correct?

A Wilma only

B Tuan only

C Both Wilma and Tuan

D Neither Wilma nor Tuan

Question 24

A corner reflector is created when three square mirrors are placed at right angles. Light hitting any of the mirrors is reflected back in the direction from where it came.

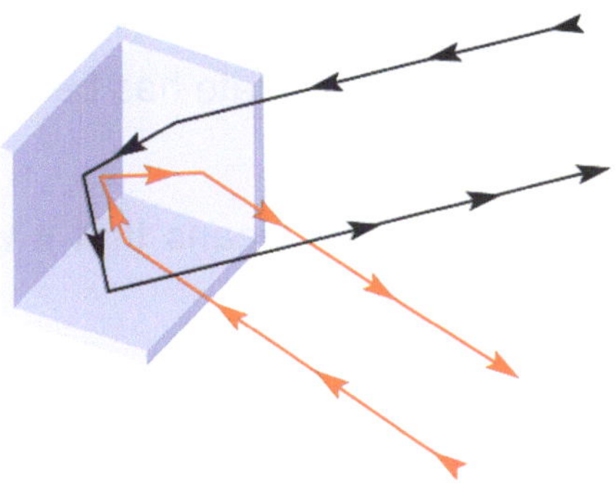

Additional information

- Light tends to scatter as it travels through air.
- As light scatters its intensity weakens.
- Laser light scatters very little.

Stan says: "If one of these is placed on the Moon, we can know how far away the Moon is from the Earth."

Stacey replies: "If we use strong lasers, these reflectors can be useful to show drivers at night where the edges of unlit roads are."

Which of the following is **incorrect** based on the information?

A If Stan is right then we need to know the speed of light and have a good timer as well.

B If Stacey is right then headlights should be behind the driver's head, not at the front of the car.

C If Stan is right then Stacey is right about the use of lasers.

D If Stacey is right then headlights spread light quite broadly.

Question 25

> When the car has an orange spanner showing on the dashboard it means the car needs to be serviced.

The orange light can come on when a pre-set date has been reached or when a number of kilometres has been driven.

Hubert: "The orange light is flashing which means that it will soon be time to service the car."

Lionel: "It is flashing so it is warning that the service is overdue."

If the information in the box is true, whose reasoning is correct?

A Hubert only

B Lionel only

C Both Hubert and Lionel

D Neither Hubert nor Lionel

Question 26

Vivian and Jodie wanted to find out which sports were most favoured in their class. They did a survey of the students in the class and found the following:

- Everyone who liked handball also liked basketball.
- Some people liked both basketball and cricket.
- No-one liked both cricket and handball.
- There were more people who only liked basketball than people who only liked cricket.
- All of those who liked athletics also liked handball.

Which was the most popular sport?

A Handball

B Basketball

C Cricket

D Athletics

Question 27

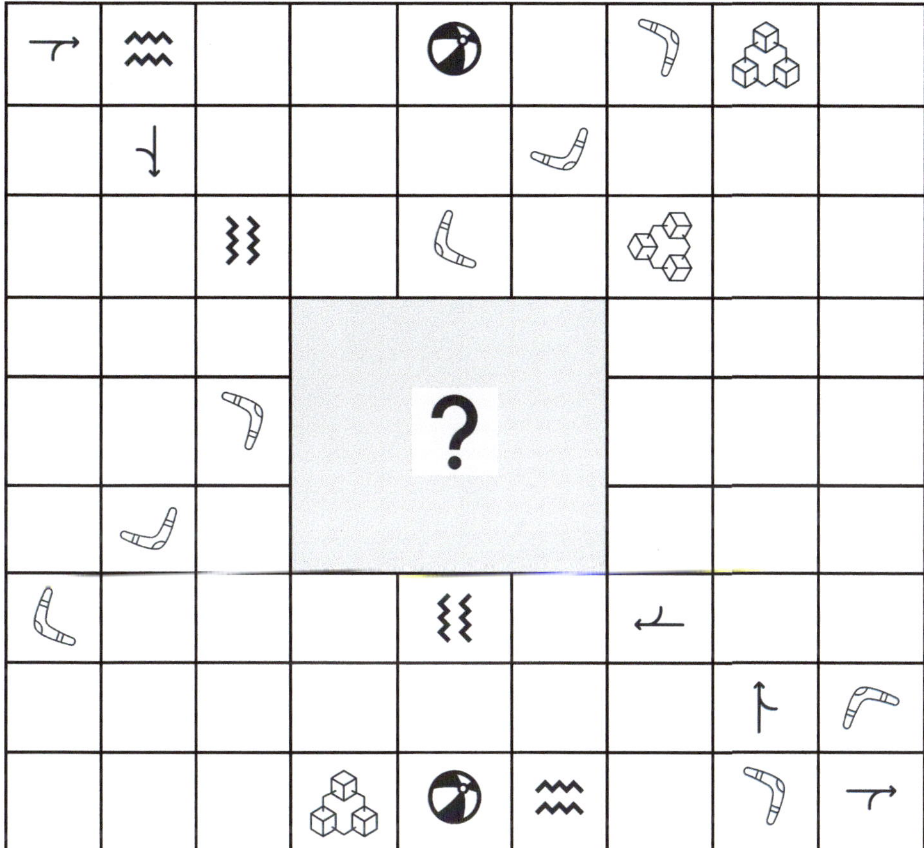

Which of these represents the missing pattern?

A

B

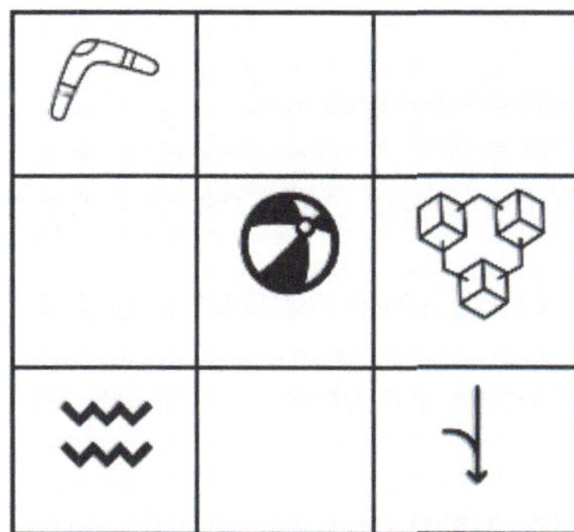

C

D

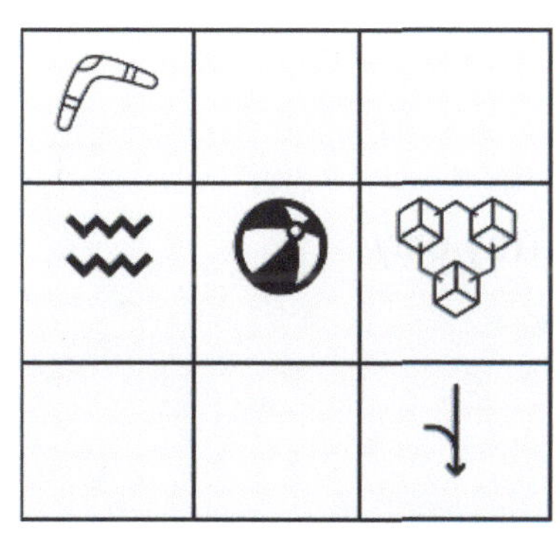

Question 28

Best before: Means a product has its highest quality before this date.

Use by: This is the expiry date and products should not be consumed after this date.

On 11th of December Natasha drank some of the refrigerated drink below and was fine. On the 14th of December Natasha drank the rest of the refrigerated drink and felt sick afterwards.

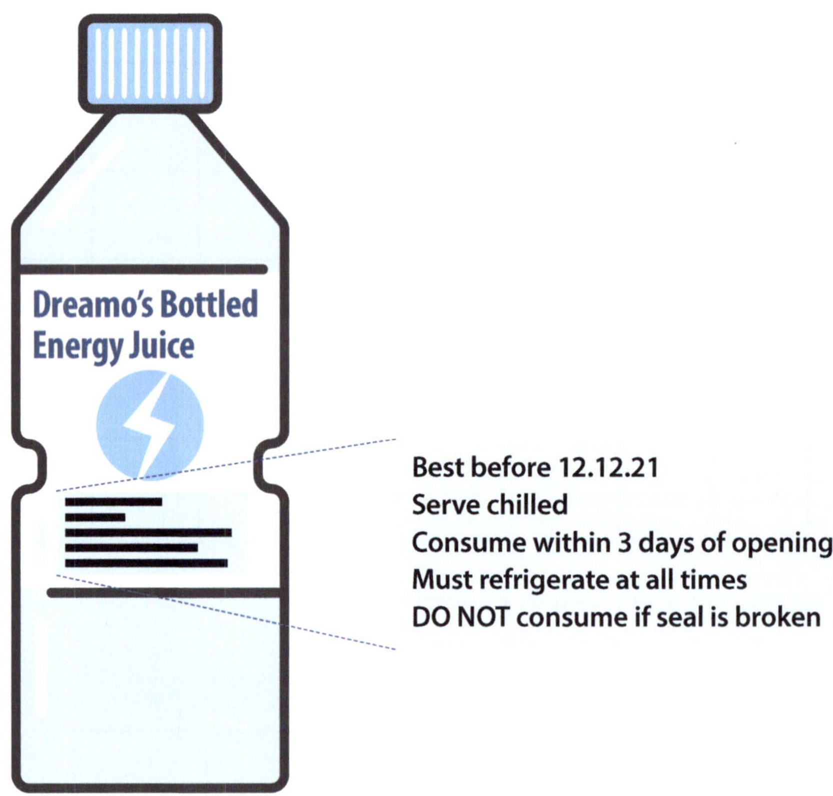

Denise: "It must have been past its use by date!"

Natasha: "I should not have consumed it after I broke the seal."

Troy: "You should have finished it earlier in the day."

Based on the information provided, whose reasoning is **most** correct?

A Troy only

B Natasha only

C Natasha and Troy only

D Denise only

Question 29

Six children did a test with five difficult questions to answer.

- Corey was first to finish and got two questions wrong.
- Brian got all the questions right but took second longest.
- Ngoli was second fastest and got one more question wrong than Mee.
- Jung finished faster than Trae and Brian and did as well as Mee.
- Mee, who got two questions wrong, was faster than Jung but slower than Corey.
- Trae did not get the lowest score.

If every one of the above statements is true, only one of the sentences below **cannot** be true. Which one?

A Mee finished third.

B Trae and Ngoli got the lowest score.

C Trae did as well as Brian.

D Ngoli got the lowest score.

Question 30

A test has been designed to assess whether salt can be used as a preservative for cooked potatoes.

Four dishes of cooked potatoes are made, and two questions are asked in each case.

Cooked Dish	Was salt added to the cooked potatoes?	Was the cooked potato preserved?
1	No	(a)
2	(b)	No
3	Yes	(c)
4	(d)	No

Which **two** of the missing answers **must** be known in order to test whether salt can be used as an effective preservative for cooked potatoes?

A (a) and (b)

B (a) and (c)

C (b) and (c)

D (c) and (d)

Question 31

Vera was to buy 6 singlets. There are four different shops that sell the singlets she wants. The shops, the price of the singlets and any discounts, sales promotions and special offers are listed in the table:

Shop	Regular singlet price	Discounts, sales promotions and special offers
Warm Body	$16	Buy 2, get a third free
Singlets'R'us	$13	Buy 2, get 50% off a third
Cool Cotton	$14	Buy 1, get the next at half price
No Sleeves	$15	Members buy: $8.50 each. Membership cost: $13

If Vera wants to buy all her singlets from one shop and wants to spend the least amount of money, where should she buy her singlets from?

A Warm Body

B Singlets'R'us

C Cool Cotton

D No Sleeves

Question 32

Even though many people do not know it, running is good for your knees. Many non-runners say that running on paved surfaces is bad for leg joints but this is not shown in scientific studies. A high proportion of doctors will tell patients with arthritis that they should not run as it will worsen the condition, but this is based on anecdote as the science does not bear this out. Barefoot runners like paved surfaces and also grassed surfaces. Improvements in shoe technologies lessen the impacts on feet, knees and hips.

Which one of the following statements, if true, most **strengthens** the above argument?

A Runners should only run on soft surfaces or with very good shoes.

B People with knee and joint problems should run.

C Many people run through slight or moderate pain.

D Regular and repeated joint movement reduces the effects of arthritis.

Question 33

160 people were asked to identify their favourite colour. The results are shown in the table.

Only these fours colours were chosen.

	Purple	69
	Blue	51
	Red	29
	Black	11

The information was entered into a computer in order to construct a pie chart. However, one of the colours was accidentally left out. Consequently, this was the pie chart that appeared on the screen.

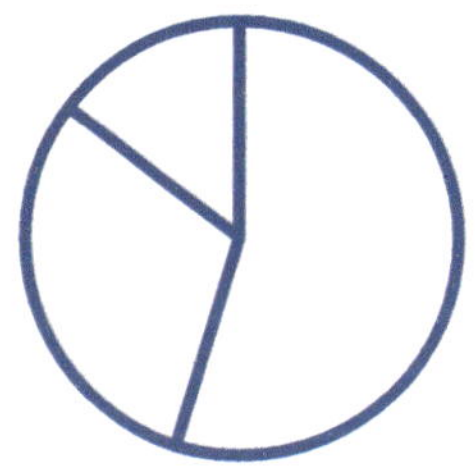

Which of the colours had been accidentally left out?

A Purple

B Blue

C Red

D Black

Question 34

A chocolate is hidden in one of three boxes. On the lid of each box, two statements are written. Each statement may be true, or it may be false. However, no more than one statement on each lid is false.

Box 1	Box 2	Box 3
The chocolate is square.	The chocolate is round.	The chocolate is not in this Box.
The chocolate is not in this box.	The chocolate is not in Box 1.	The chocolate is in Box 2.

Which one of the following statements must be true?

A The chocolate is square.

B The chocolate is round.

C The chocolate is in Box 2.

D The chocolate is in Box 3.

Question 35

Coffee is healthier than tea. It is much better than tea as a stimulus due to its high caffeine content. Studies show that caffeine stimulates the production of adrenalin in the body. Adrenalin is used by the body to energise and to ready the body for 'fight or flight' responses. It therefore makes the body alert. Studies have also linked coffee to lower incidences of Alzheimer's disease and Parkinson's disease.

Which one of the following statements, if true, most **weakens** the above argument?

A More people globally drink tea than coffee.

B Tea comes in wider varieties than coffee.

C Tea drinkers report feeling good after drinking tea regularly.

D Tea contains antioxidants which boost the immune system.

Question 36

Selena visited the pony show and saw 10 pony owners displaying their ponies.

Some of the pony owners had 1 pony, some had 2 and one had 3 ponies.

Counting all of the legs of the ponies and the pony owners, there was a total of 92 legs.

Each pony has 4 legs, and all pony owners have 2 legs.

How many pony owners had 2 ponies?

A 9

B 6

C 4

D 3

Question 37

In order to enter the State poetry slam competition, a student must have won two school poetry competitions or won a regional competition.

Seven students from Nabila's school have been accepted as entrants for the State poetry slam competition.

Nabila says, "I know that students at our school won 8 school poetry competitions. This means that 3 of them must have won a regional competition."

Which of the following sentences shows the **mistake** Nabila has made?

A Some students who won school competitions also won a regional competition.

B There has been a big increase in the number of poetry competitions held this year.

C Some students won only 1 school competition.

D Some students may have won 2 or more regional competitions.

Question 38

A group of scientists wanted to test the speed of flying insects. This is what they found:

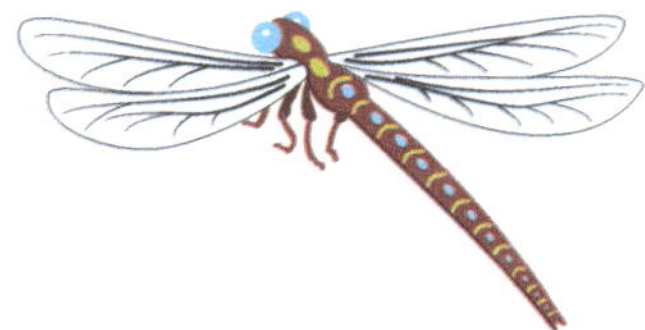

- The fastest dragonflies were faster than the fastest moths.
- All of the horseflies were faster than most of the dragonflies.
- All of the moths were faster than all of the horseflies.

Which one of these can be **concluded** from the above information?

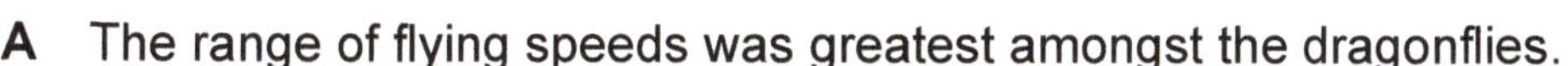

A The range of flying speeds was greatest amongst the dragonflies.

B Dragonflies and moths will generally be faster than horseflies.

C The average dragonfly is faster than the average moth.

D The range of flying speeds amongst horseflies was greater than the range of flying speeds amongst moths.

Question 39

Marcel, David, Janice and Petra all play a computer game called ***Maya.***

- David's average score is higher than Marcel's average score.
- Janice's lowest score is higher than Petra's lowest score.
- Marcel's lowest score is higher than Janice's highest score.
- Janice's lowest score is higher than David's ten lowest scores.

What can be **concluded** from the information provided?

A David's average score is higher than Janice's average score.

B Marcel's average score is higher than Petra's average score.

C Petra has the lowest average score.

D Petra has the highest average score.

Question 40

Rodney's football coach says that whoever in the squad was not chosen in the first four games will be chosen in the fifth game.

Rodney: "I played in each of the first four games so I cannot be chosen."

Which one of the following sentences shows the **mistake** that Rodney has made?

A Just because somebody from the squad is chosen for the fifth game it does not necessarily mean that they will play the game.

B Just because Rodney was chosen to play in the first four games, it does not mean that he will not be chosen in future games.

C Just because someone in the squad did not play in the first four games, it does not mean they will be available to play in the fifth game.

D Just because anyone in the squad who did not play in the first four games will play in the fifth game, it does not mean that anyone who played in the first four games will not play in the fifth game.

Answers

Summary of Answers

1	**D**	9	**A**	17	**B**	25	**D**	33	**A**
2	**C**	10	**B**	18	**C**	26	**B**	34	**C**
3	**B**	11	**D**	19	**A**	27	**C**	35	**D**
4	**C**	12	**A**	20	**D**	28	**A**	36	**B**
5	**C**	13	**A**	21	**B**	29	**B**	37	**A**
6	**D**	14	**D**	22	**B**	30	**C**	38	**A**
7	**A**	15	**C**	23	**C**	31	**C**	39	**A**
8	**A**	16	**B**	24	**B**	32	**D**	40	**D**

A = 7, 8, 9, 12, 13, 19, 28, 33, 37, 38, 39

B = 3, 10, 16, 17, 21, 22, 29, 26, 36

C = 2, 4, 5, 15, 18, 23, 27, 30, 31, 34

D = 1, 6, 11, 14, 20, 24, 25, 32, 35, 40

Fully worked solutions

Question 1

D

All of the players commence with 50 cards each.

Mai rolls a 5 which is odd. This means that she has to give each of the other two players 5 cards each.

So, Mai now has 40, Fred has 55 and Alexa has 55 cards.

Fred then rolls a 2 which is even. So, both Mai and Alexa have to give Fred 4 cards each (twice the number rolled).

So, Mai now has 36, Fred has 63 and Alexa has 51.

If Alexa ends up with 67, then she must have been given 16 cards in total, or 8 from each other player. This means she rolled a 4 and Mai gave her 8 cards (36 − 8 = 28) and Fred also gave her 8 (63 − 8 = 55).

Question 2

C

This is an argument question, so we need to (1) understand the argument and (2) make eliminations based on the grounds of any one or more of relevance, hearsay or opinion.

The argument here is that Davo is arguing that Ben does not need to give up sport. He tries to support his argument with justifications.

Of the possible answers A is an opinion. B is hearsay and D is persuasive but a general statement that relies on inductive reasoning. Deductive reasoning which applies to C is more compelling.

Question 3

B

The statement given is: "Whoever fixed the fan must have both had a ladder and a screwdriver" and the condition given is that this is true.

This means that there are two conditions for fixing the fan: having a ladder AND having a screwdriver. However, there will be millions of people who:

1. have a ladder and did not fix the fan
2. have a screwdriver and did not fix the fan
3. have a ladder and a screwdriver and did not fix the fan

The reason why we know this is because the description is particular to this situation and thus cannot be generalised. Accordingly, A must be incorrect. Furthermore, the condition is that to fix the fan a person needs certain tools – not that if a person did NOT fix the fan they do not have tools, thus C and D are incorrect.

What is known for certain is what has been given: a person without a ladder cannot have fixed the fan, just as a person without a screwdriver cannot have fixed the fan. Hence B is correct.

Question 4

C

We know that at least one of the men is lying. So, assume that the bald man is telling the truth. If he loves Chai Latte then the long-haired man must also be telling the truth as we know they each must love a different tea. However, both cannot be telling the truth thus A cannot be correct.

This is the same situation presented by B as if the man is not lying then he is telling the truth and if that is the case then so is the bald man. Thus B is incorrect.

If the long-haired man does not love Chai Latte – as in D – then it means he loves Dandelion tea. This would mean he is telling the truth, so we have the same situation as in A and B.

If one of the men is lying then the other one must also be lying as they both love a different tea, hence C must be correct.

Question 5

C

Look at all the possible numbers that could be represented below from 2 to 9. Since two of the segments do not work they must be the segments denoted in **RED** making the two digits 4 and 5:

The next digit must therefore be 6:

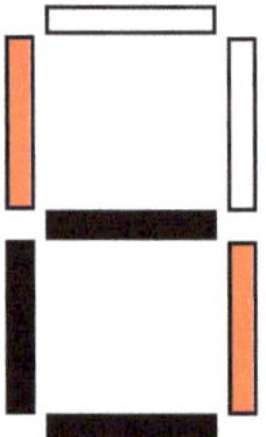

Hence C is correct.

Question 6

D

We know that Albert takes longer than 15 minutes to get to work. We therefore know the conditions are not the best: it may be rainy, he may have left between 8AM and 9AM – or both may have occurred. Just because it was not sunny does not necessarily mean it is rainy – it could be cloudy. Thus, A can be discounted. We do not know what time leaving home would be 'late' thus B must be eliminated. We do not know when Albert drove thus C cannot be correct. We do know that at least one of two factors must have been present: either it was rainy or Albert drove to work between 8AM – 9AM. Hence D is correct.

Question 7

A

Here we need to establish an order and then determine when each child is born. Since Han was born 2 months before Dwight we write this: **H X D**

If Ravi is 5 months younger than Han then he must have been born later in the year so now we know this: **H X D X X R**

Since Vuong and Leo are born in the same month we now write this placing them below the list:

H X D X X R

V
L

Since Leo was born in August and so was Vuong we now write this:

H X D X X R

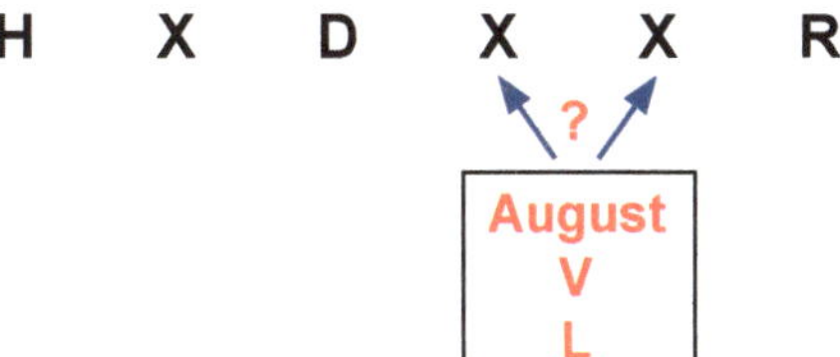

Now, Aaron is younger than Dwight and older than one other person, and was not born in the same month as anyone else. This means that Aaron must be next to Ravi and that is September:

The order MUST be: **H X D V, L (August) A R**

Hence we know that Dwight was born in July, Aaron was born in September, Ravi was born in October and Aaron was born AFTER Vuong (and Leo). Hence A is correct.

Question 8

A

Start with what is known and work logically and in order:

Firstly, there are 264 female ostriches but 10 have no chicks so we know that 254 do have chicks.

Secondly, one has three chicks meaning that 360 – 3 = 357 chicks were born to 253 female ostriches that have either one or two chicks.

Thirdly, since all of these 253 ostriches had AT LEAST one chick we know that 357 – 253 must have had TWO chicks.

That is, 104 ostriches had TWO chicks. This means that 253 – 104 = 149 must have had 1 chick. So, 149 ostriches have exactly 1 chick.

We can check as follows: (149 × 1) + (104 × 2) + 3 must equal 360. 149 + 208 + 3 = 360 hence A must be correct.

Question 9

A

The main thing to remember here is that February can have either 28 days or it can have 29 days in a leap year. This means that the 29th day after January finished may be February 29th OR March 1st – depending on whether the year is a leap year or not.

Accordingly, two weeks after it was bought, if it was a leap year, it would be 14th March so that can be true. Since the bicycle could have been purchased on 29th February C can also be true. If it was not a leap year then 29 days after January would be March 1st so D can also be true. However, A cannot be true as Jason rode the bike on the day he got it – not the day after. It was first used in the same month it was bought.

Question 10

B

The main argument that Pritipath has here is that electric cars lack reliability. So, the statement must reinforce this aspect. A cannot be the strongest supporting statement as the distance ("far") has not been quantified, nor the number ("many"). C implies that weight can slow cars down but there has been no link shown between the weight of batteries and the reliability of electric cars hence it must be discounted. D is irrelevant as the argument is not one about price or cost.

B directly relates to this statement made by Pritipath: **without enough places to recharge they are not reliable**. Hence B, which refers to the lack of places to charge, strengthens his argument.

Answers

Question 11

D

The issue here is that Robert has assumed the data sets are mutually exclusive instead of overlapping.

We know that 8 prizes will be given out as there are three prize winners in each of two age categories: 6 runners will get place prizes.

However, any of those people may also have been one of the two who ran faster than 3 minutes and thirty seconds per kilometre. Hence as few as 6 or 7 runners could get medals – not necessarily 8. Hence D indicates his error.

A is incorrect as Robert's error (D) was not to do with individuals who run one kilometre faster than 3 minutes 30 seconds. B is a distractor as the question is not how easy or difficult running a particular speed is – it is about whether a person who is a placegetter could also have met the time requirement. C is irrelevant as the number of persons in the race or age groups is not really a factor unless there happened to be only 6 or 7 participants in total. However, this reasoning changes the premise of the question rather than applying logic to the information given.

Question 12

A

We know that the conditions are that a person requires three particular strengths:

1. be mathematically brilliant
2. have perfect sight
3. be able to multitask

Accordingly, a person cannot have glasses or wear contact lenses so Josie cannot be correct. Therefore, C must be incorrect. Amira states that Lomu forgets basic number rules – a fundamental aspect of mathematics and unequivocally Lomu cannot be a pilot. Amira is equivocal rather than emphatic - hence B can be eliminated. Davis makes a statement that recognises 2 of the 3 strengths in Serena – but we do not know anything about her sight so we cannot be sure that she can even become a pilot. Hence D can be eliminated, and A must be correct.

Question 13

A

This can be drawn and numbered as follows:

1	2	3	4	5	6

We know there are three women: Katy, Vesna and Wendy and three men: Mark, Steve and David.

The men sit on odd numbered seats and the women on even numbered seats so we can write this:

1M	2W	3M	4W	5M	6W

We cannot yet action any of these:

- Each person owns and drives a car.
- Three cars are black, one is silver, one red and one blue.
- Katy drives a black car.

So, we move on to this:
Mark is four seats to the left of David thus David MUST be in Seat 5 and Mark in Seat 1. This also means that Steve must be in Seat 3.

1M Mark	2W	3M Steve	4W	5M David	6W

We cannot action these yet:

- One of the women has a red car.
- David's car is not black or blue.

So we move to these:

- The women sit in reverse alphabetical order.
- One person beside Mark drives a red car.

1M Mark	2W Wendy Red Car	3M Steve	4W Vesna	5M David	6W Katy

We can now revisit what has been missed:

- Three cars are black, one is silver, one red and one blue.
- Katy drives a black car.
- One of the women has a red car and one of the men has a blue car.
- David's car is not black or blue.

1M Mark	2W Wendy Red Car	3M Steve	4W Vesna	5M David	6W Katy Black Car

Since David does not have a black or blue car, and since Wendy has a red car then David's car must be silver. Moreover, since one of the men has a blue car then we know Vesna's car must be black.

1M Mark	2W Wendy Red Car	3M Steve	**4W Vesna Black Car**	5M David Silver Car	6W Katy Black Car

We now know for certain who is sitting in Seat 4 and the colour of car the person has: Vesna who drives a black car, hence the answer is A.

Question 14

D

The pieces fit as shown below so the missing piece is D.

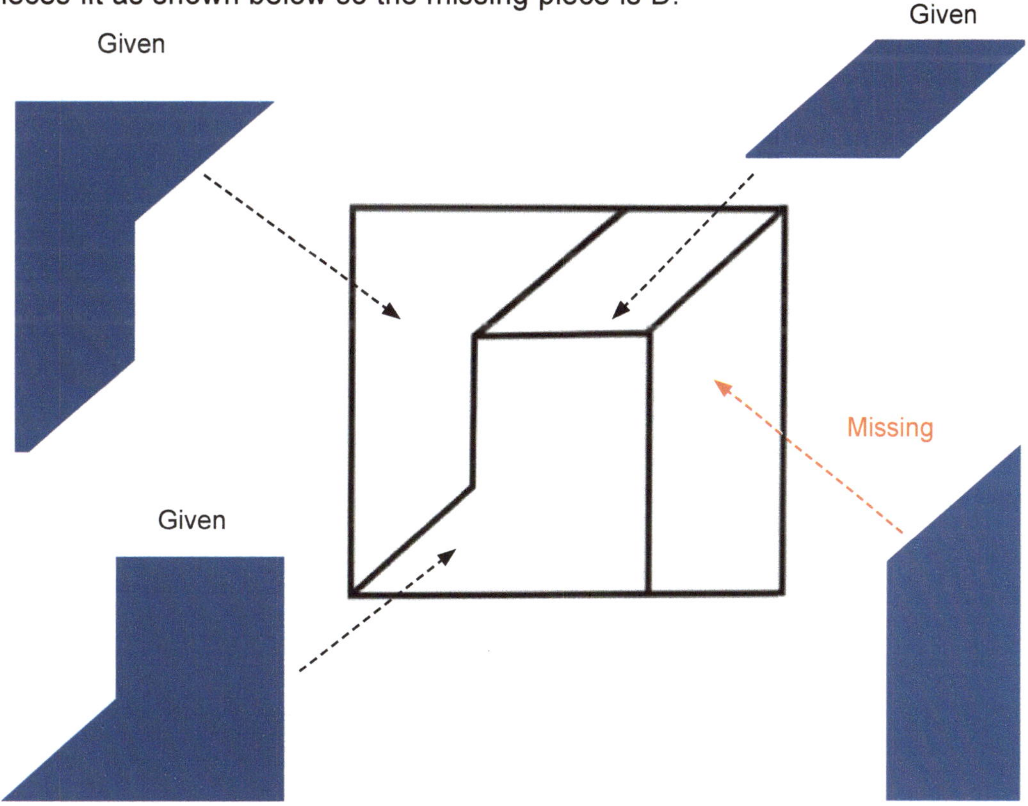

Question 15

C

Here students need to quickly identify the closest top marks (shown in bold) and actually do not need to calculate the rest (though they are shown). Now Alira is clearly leading on 96 and the second highest is Ratnayke on 85. This is a full 11 marks behind Alira. So, if Alira scores 89 or less, she opens herself up to being beaten by Ratnayke or, depending on what she gets, even Justyn, Warren or Nancy. Thus, to ensure she wins the prize Alira must get 90 marks.

Name	Test 1 Mark	Test 2 Mark	Total of test 1 and 2 (out of 100)
Nancy	38	43	81
Ratnayke	**47**	**38**	**85**
Zoe	35	34	69
Warren	41	40	81
Khuong	27	34	61
Lam	40	38	78
Andrew	28	29	57
Lilith	33	33	66
Nicholas	39	40	79
Peter	31	27	58
Cindy	37	36	73
Justyn	42	41	83
Jacqueline	29	33	62
Alira	**49**	**47**	**96**

Question 16

B

We know that each tile is identical – but they do not look the same. This means there must be a rotation. In this shape the quarter circle is opposite the spike and the elbow is opposite the triangle corner (see below):

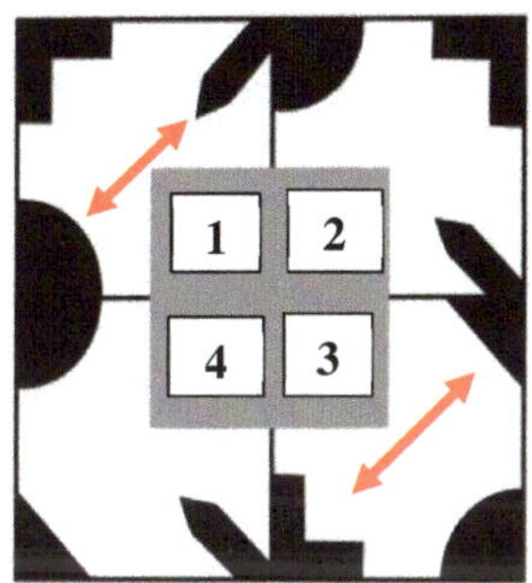

Thus, the missing shape must have a triangle at 1 and 2 (opposite the elbow), a spike at 3 and an elbow at 4. This is shown in B.

Question 17

B

HINT: Read all the information and then we can take a couple of steps at a time.

Let us start with what we know:
There are five places which can be represented as boxes or crosses. Here we will use crosses:

X X X X X

As Simon finished ahead of three other cars we can do this:

X Leon (Silver) X X (Black) X Simon X (Green car)

We can also mark each of the following:

- Simon's car, which is not green or red, finished ahead of three others.
- The green car came first.
- When Leon finished in his silver car there were four cars ahead of him.
- The black car finished third.

We can now take the third step:
There are two cars between Stephanie and Anna. Given this we can now know that Stephanie must be fourth and Anna must be first:

X Leon (Silver) X (Stephanie) X (Black) - EMILY X Simon X (Green car) Anna

Finally, we can do this:
Emily, in a black car, was behind Anna: thus, Emily must be third and in the black car. Hence B must be correct.

Question 18

C

The main argument here is that fire behaviour needs to be understood. A is not relevant to this argument and can be discounted. B is also not directly relevant as it is a statement about firefighters not about fires. Whilst firefighters are better trained this may mean they understand fire behaviour better but it can also mean that they are 'catching up' as the fires are changing to become more intense and harder to manage. Hence B can be eliminated.

D is hearsay and therefore not useful.

C is relevant as this knowledge strengthens the argument that fires and their behaviour need to be understood. Since native trees have oils that affect how fire behaves this is directly relevant to the argument.

Question 19

A

Nadia is standing on the X and facing North. As she turns, she will see three layers. The layers will look either like A or C. However, if the triangles are all prisms then the corners are also edges. Hence A will be a more accurate depiction.

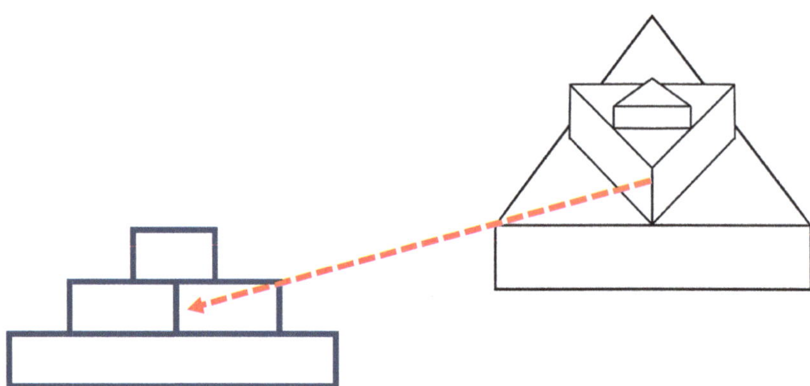

Question 20

D

Given that this information in the box is true then the word **ONLY** is crucial.

The seahorse is a Hippocampus and is the **only** fish where the male bears the unborn young.

It means that Ngoc's statement must be true as the only male fish that can bear young is a seahorse. Hence, A and C can be eliminated. Stacy is also correct as her premise is any fish bearing young which is NOT a seahorse – cannot be male. If it cannot be male, then it must be female which is true if ONLY male seahorses bear live young. All other fish, who are female, bear young.

Hence D must be correct.

Question 21

B

Donna must buy a 3-month movie pass which means she can watch 8 movies in the next 2 months. She must then buy 2 of the $20 passes to watch 3 more per month making the total $50 + $20 + $20 = $90.

Question 22

B

There are three conditions that apply for a cricket ball to swing and one or more may apply:

- It is bowled faster than 130 km per hour.
- One side of the ball is smooth, and the other side is rough.
- The ball is held with the seam on an angle.

Ashlee says: "The seam was vertical, so it must have been bowled at over 130 km per hour." In saying this she is saying that the ball was not held with the seam on an angle. That eliminates the third condition so C can be discounted. We are not told how fast the ball was bowled or if it has a rough side. Hence A cannot be certain, and B is possible – thus B must be correct.

D is not relevant as it refers to factors outside of consideration.

Question 23

C

Take Wilma's statement first, where an object is changing its direction (her hand). At every point on a path inscribed by an object moving in a circle the direction of motion is changing as shown below:

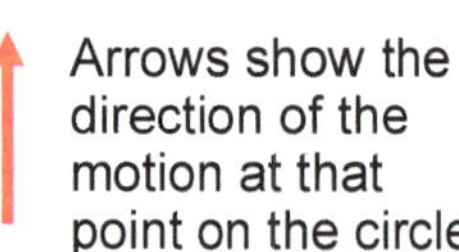

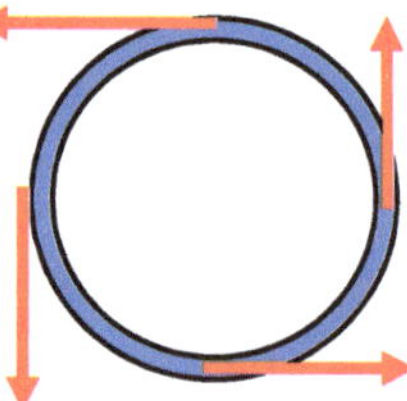

Hence BOTH are correct, and the answer is C.

Question 24

B

The stimulus indicates that the light will return in the direction of the source. Here there are three important pieces of information in addition to the stimulus. From the additional information we know that light will spread out in air, meaning ordinary light will be reflected more widely than the light coming from the source. The exception will be laser light.

In order to determine the distance from the Moon to the Earth we need to know the speed of light and the time it takes to get to the Moon and back. Consequently, A will be correct. Since lasers do not scatter much light then C is also correct. Since car headlights will need to cover a wide area then the reflected light from a corner reflector would be visible to drivers – hence D is also correct.

B is incorrect as even in the event where light is spread very little, all that is required is for the headlights to be in line with the driver's eyes, not behind the driver's head.

Question 25

D

All that is known is the orange spanner light comes on if a car needs servicing. We do not know what a flashing light means. Consequently, the reasoning of both Hubert and Lionel is not correct, and hence D is correct.

Question 26

B

This can be drawn as a Venn Diagram and can also be determined through the application of logical reasoning. Start by numbering the information:

1. Everyone who liked handball also liked basketball.
2. Some people liked both basketball and cricket.
3. No-one liked both cricket and handball.
4. There were more people who only liked basketball than people who only liked cricket.
5. All of those who liked athletics also liked handball.

If all those who liked athletics also liked handball (5) and all those who like handball liked basketball (1) then all those who like handball also like basketball. In addition, since more people only liked basketball than those who only liked cricket (4) then basketball MUST be more popular that cricket. However, basketball is liked by all those who like athletics and handball, so it must be at LEAST as popular as both these sports. Since basketball has additional admirers it must be most popular.

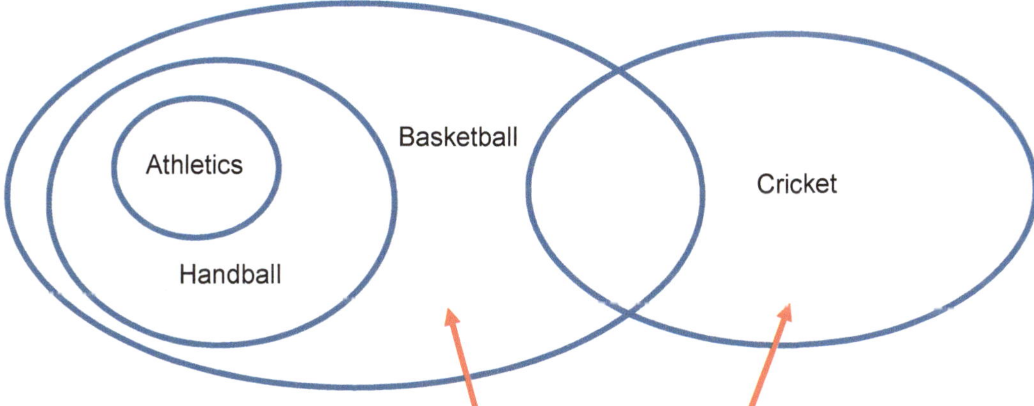

This area is larger than this area as (4) applies

Question 27

C

The movement of each of the symbols is shown in red below.

Note the rotation of each of the symbols except the ball.

Note also that the ↾ symbol will be covered by other symbols when they occupy the same square.

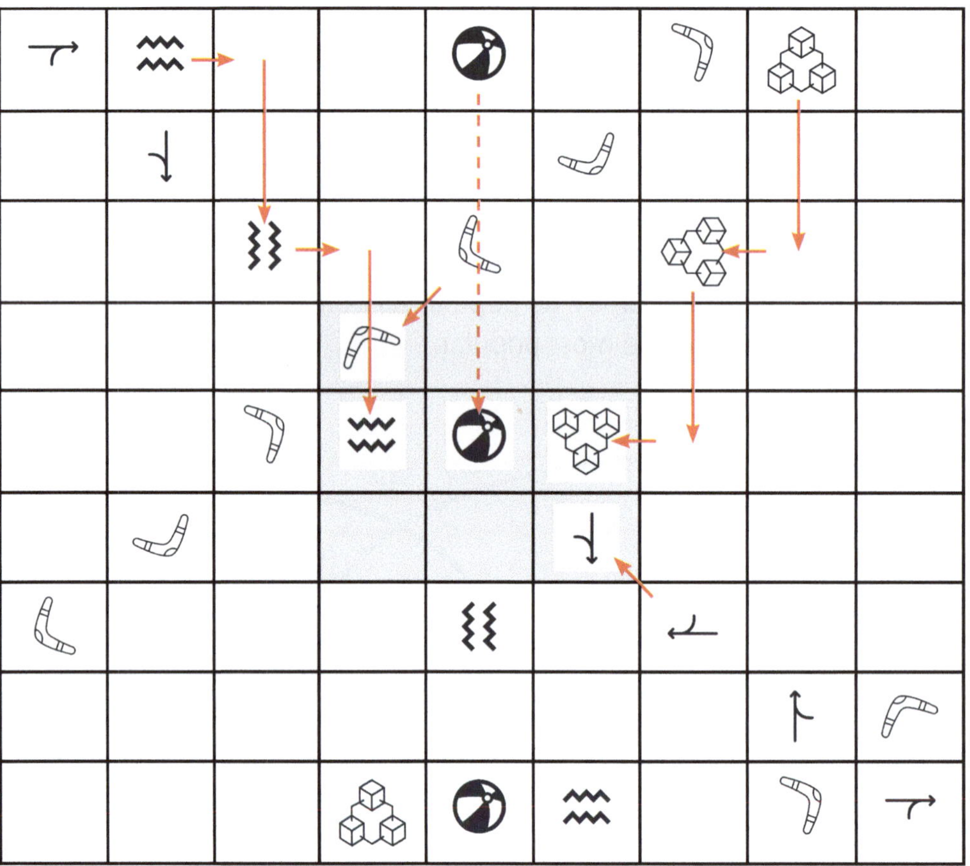

It will look like this:

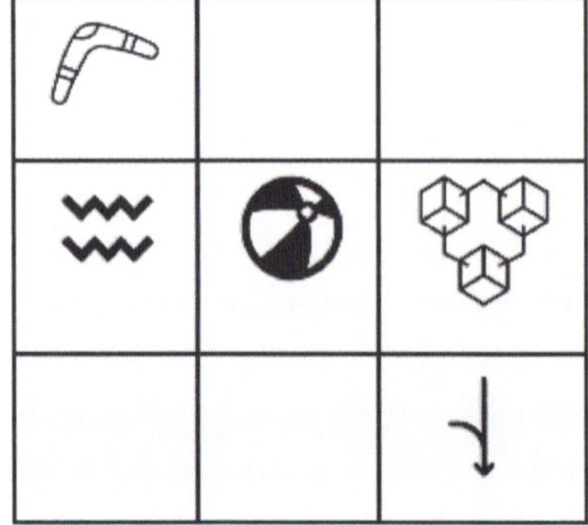

Question 28

A

The information given is as follows:

> **Best before 12.12.21**
> **Serve chilled**
> **Consume within 3 days of opening**
> **Must refrigerate at all times**
> **DO NOT consume if seal is broken**

We do not know the use by date so we can discount Denise's response and eliminate D. Natasha cannot be correct as there are two pieces of information – one of which qualifies the other: if the seal is broken prior to its use then the product should not be consumed. This is because we do not know if it would be safe to drink. However, once we know when the seal is broken, as long as the product is refrigerated, it should last 3 days (72 hours). Hence B and C can be eliminated.

Troy's reasoning, A is the **most** correct as he has considered the possibility of the time across 11th – 14th December surpassing the time of 3 days (for example, opening the drink on the morning of the 11th and finishing it on the afternoon of the 14th).

Question 29

B

Step by step: (1) Corey was first to finish and got two questions wrong.

Finishing order	6	5	4	3	2	**1 Corey**
Number correct out of 5						3

(2) Brian got all the questions right but took second longest

Finishing order	6	**5 Brian**	4	3	2	1 Corey
Number correct out of 5		5				3

(3) Ngoli was second fastest and got one more question wrong than Mee

Finishing order	6	5 Brian	4	3	**2 Ngoli**	1 Corey
Number correct out of 5		5				3

(4) Jung finished faster than Trae and Brian and did as well as Mee

Finishing order	**6 Trae**	5 Brian	**4 Jung**	3	2 Ngoli	1 Corey
Number correct out of 5		5				3

(5) Mee, who got two questions wrong, was faster than Jung but slower than Corey

Finishing order	6 Trae	5 Brian	4 Jung	**3 Mee**	2 Ngoli	1 Corey
Number correct out of 5		5	3 (from Step 4)	3	2 (from Step 3)	3

(6) Trae did not get the lowest score

Finishing order	6 Trae	5 Brian	4 Jung	3 Mee	2 Ngoli	1 Corey
Number correct out of 5	3, 4 or 5	5	3	3	2	3

We now know that Mee was **either** equal second or equal third as we do not know if Trae got 3, 4 or 5. Hence A can be true. We do not know what Trae scored and he could have got 3, 4 or 4 (as did Brian) thus C can be true. Ngoli who scored 2 got the lowest score so D is also true and can be eradicated. However B cannot be true as Trae got at least 3. Hence the answer is B.

Question 30

C

Here we need to know whether the addition of salt preserves or not. The four options that are covered are shown in **RED** in the table below. This covers all of the permutations.

Cooked Dish	Was salt added to the cooked potatoes?	Was the cooked potato preserved?
1	No	(a) or YES
2	(b) or NO	No
3	Yes	(c) or YES
4	(d) or YES	No

The two answers that must be known are (b) and (c) because if salt is *NOT* added as in (a) and the potato is preserved then we cannot know when salt *IS ADDED* whether the preservative effect is from the salt. Moreover, we must also know that (d) must be wrong as if salt is added and the potatoes are not preserved then we do not know whether it can preserve or not, or how much needs to be added.

Question 31

C

A new column has been added to show the calculations. Cool Cotton, or C is the lowest price.

Shop	Regular singlet price	Discounts, sales promotions and special offers	Total cost of 6 singlets
Warm Body	$16	Buy 2, get a third free	($16 × 2) × 2 = $64
Singlets'R'us	$13	Buy 2, get 50% off a third	[($13 × 2) + $6.50] × 2 = $65
Cool Cotton	$14	Buy 1, get the next at half price	($14 + $14/2) × 3 = $21 × 3 = $63
No Sleeves	$15	Members buy: $8.50 each. Membership cost: $13	($8.50 × 6) + $13 = $51 + $13 = $64

Question 32

D

The central argument here is that running is good for the joints. Thus to strengthen the argument the option must support this. A is not supported by the passage and can be used to counter the argument that running is beneficial hence A can be discounted. There is no element of compulsion in the argument posed so the notion that people with knee and joint problems 'should' does not enter the argument. Indeed, it is irrelevant. C represents an opinion and thus does not strengthen the argument. If D is true, then it compellingly boosts the argument and thus it is correct.

Question 33

A

The long-hand way to do this is shown in the Table below.

	Purple	69	Missing	69 or 63%	69 or 53%	69 or 46%
	Blue	51	51 or 56%	Missing	51 or 39%	51 or 34%
	Red	29	29 or 32%	29 or 26%	Missing	29 or 19%
	Black	11	11 or 12%	11 or 10%	11 or 8%	Missing
	TOTALS	**160**	**91**	**109**	**131**	**149**

However, problem-solvers only need to look carefully at the pie chart to see that the largest number is in the order of 55% of the total. The smallest segment is close to half of a quarter (this is evident visually) thus 12% would be closest and hence purple must be the forgotten colour.

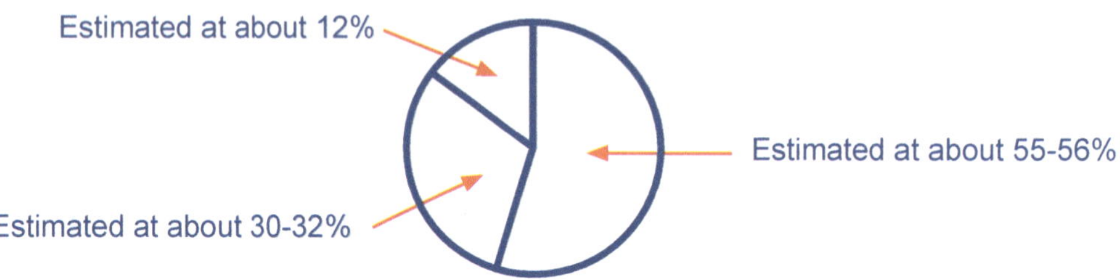

Question 34

C

Test each statement and ask "if this is false" is the other statement necessarily also false? This is the key to this question as no more than ONE statement on each box can be false.

Look at Box 3

If the first statement, "**The chocolate is not in this Box**" is false the chocolate MUST be in Box 3. However, if this is the case then the second statement must also be false as the chocolate CANNOT be in Box 2.

Hence these statements MUST both be true, and the chocolate is in Box 2.

Box 1	Box 2	Box 3
The chocolate is square.	The chocolate is round.	The chocolate is not in this Box.
The chocolate is not in this box.	The chocolate is not in Box 1.	The chocolate is in Box 2.

Question 35

D

The argument here is that coffee is healthier than tea so any counter argument will either point to coffee being less healthy than tea or will point out the health benefits of tea.

A is not relevant as the number of tea drinkers is not relevant to health effects. B is also irrelevant as the argument is not about variety or range. C is hearsay and can be discarded. It does not strengthen the argument. D points to health effects associated with tea and thus weakens the argument that coffee is healthier than tea.

Question 36

B

Step 1
Start with what is known: there are 10 pony owners and each of them has 2 legs. Thus, the pony owners have 20 legs in total. This means that the ponies must have 72 legs collectively.

The total number of ponies must be 72 ÷ 4 = 18 ponies.

Step 2
1 owner has 3 ponies so the other 9 owners must have 15 ponies in total.

Step 3
Since ALL of these owners have at least one pony then 6 of them must have 2 ponies. This is because 15 – 9 = 6 (meaning 6 of the 9 have a second pony).

Hence B is correct.

Question 37

A

Consider the following: if 7 students from Nabila's school won a regional competition (but won ZERO school poetry competitions) – how many students from the school can be accepted as entrants for the State poetry slam? Herein lies the issue with Nabila's reasoning. Since the statement is written as either/or then the second condition is NOT contingent on the first condition. They are separate criteria.

It is possible that 1 student won all of the 8 school poetry competitions, or in this case 2 as Nabila uses the plural, "students".

So, now to the options: B is irrelevant and can be dismissed. The number of regional competitions won by any student is immaterial as a student only needs to win 1 and the logic in this question turns on the number of school poetry competition victories. Hence D can be dismissed as well.

If a student won a school-based competition, they will not have been chosen, so C can be dismissed.

A is correct as it is possible for a student to have won both school poetry competitions and also a regional competition.

Question 38

A

Taking the information given, we can number the bullet points as follows:

1. The fastest dragonflies were faster than the fastest moths.
2. All of the horseflies were faster than most of the dragonflies.
3. All of the moths were faster than all of the horseflies.

Reading them all carefully, we can start with statement (3) as this gives us a comparison that is definite: Moths will generally be faster than horseflies. We can therefore draw this:

Moths

Horseflies

We now look at the dragonflies – or statement 2: All of the horseflies were faster than most of the dragonflies so we can represent this as follows:

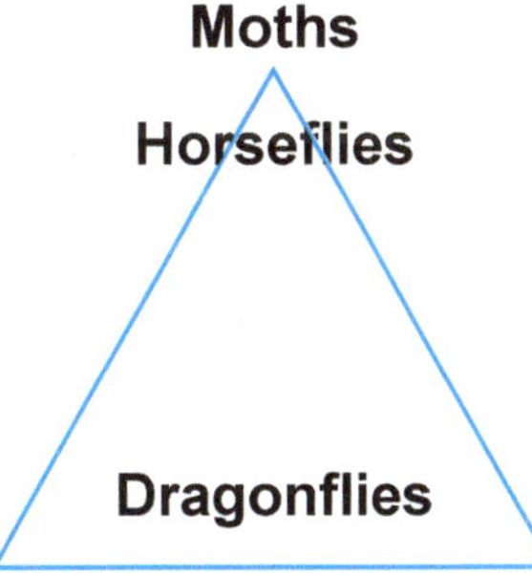

Now we look at statement 1. The fastest dragonflies were faster than the fastest moths, so the triangle can now be extended further:

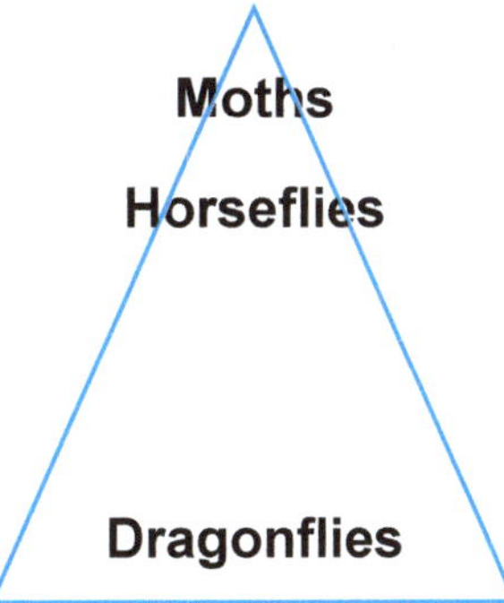

It should now be clear that B is incorrect as generally dragonflies will be slowest. C is also clearly incorrect. D is not evident from the data but A can definitely be concluded.

Question 39

A

Number the bullet points as follows:

1. David's average score is higher than Marcel's average score.
2. Janice's lowest score is higher than Petra's lowest score.
3. Marcel's lowest score is higher than Janice's highest score.
4. Janice's lowest score is higher than David's ten lowest scores.

We know that since David's average score is higher than Marcel's average score from statement 1. We also know that Marcel's lowest score is higher than Janice's highest score from (3), therefore Marcel's average score must be higher than Janice's average score. It also follows that David's average score must be higher than Janice's average score as well. Thus, A is correct.

There is not enough information to justify any of the other answers.

Question 40

D

Here the focus is on those who are in the squad who have not yet played a game. The assumption made by Rodney is that anyone who has previously played (in any of the first four games) cannot be chosen for the fifth game. But this is not the condition. There may be only one player in the squad who has not played in any of the first four games, so only one person, in that instance would be replaced – and ALL the rest would play. Hence Rodney's assumption is erroneous as he has generalised.

Accordingly, A is irrelevant. C is also irrelevant as it refers to availability – not mentioned by the coach. B is not particular to game 5 and so can be discounted, but D is correct as it removes the effect of Rodney's mistaken generalisation.

Critical Thinking Skills

FOR SELECTIVE SCHOOL TESTS, OPPORTUNITY CLASS TEST AND PROBLEM SOLVING

Use pencil when filling out this sheet

Fill in the circle correctly			
●	(B)	(C)	(D)

If you make a mistake neatly cross it out and circle the correct response			
⊗	●	(C)	(D)

MULTIPLE CHOICE ANSWER SHEET

1	(A)	(B)	(C)	(D)	21	(A)	(B)	(C)	(D)
2	(A)	(B)	(C)	(D)	22	(A)	(B)	(C)	(D)
3	(A)	(B)	(C)	(D)	23	(A)	(B)	(C)	(D)
4	(A)	(B)	(C)	(D)	24	(A)	(B)	(C)	(D)
5	(A)	(B)	(C)	(D)	25	(A)	(B)	(C)	(D)
6	(A)	(B)	(C)	(D)	26	(A)	(B)	(C)	(D)
7	(A)	(B)	(C)	(D)	27	(A)	(B)	(C)	(D)
8	(A)	(B)	(C)	(D)	28	(A)	(B)	(C)	(D)
9	(A)	(B)	(C)	(D)	29	(A)	(B)	(C)	(D)
10	(A)	(B)	(C)	(D)	30	(A)	(B)	(C)	(D)
11	(A)	(B)	(C)	(D)	31	(A)	(B)	(C)	(D)
12	(A)	(B)	(C)	(D)	32	(A)	(B)	(C)	(D)
13	(A)	(B)	(C)	(D)	33	(A)	(B)	(C)	(D)
14	(A)	(B)	(C)	(D)	34	(A)	(B)	(C)	(D)
15	(A)	(B)	(C)	(D)	35	(A)	(B)	(C)	(D)
16	(A)	(B)	(C)	(D)	36	(A)	(B)	(C)	(D)
17	(A)	(B)	(C)	(D)	37	(A)	(B)	(C)	(D)
18	(A)	(B)	(C)	(D)	38	(A)	(B)	(C)	(D)
19	(A)	(B)	(C)	(D)	39	(A)	(B)	(C)	(D)
20	(A)	(B)	(C)	(D)	40	(A)	(B)	(C)	(D)

Critical Thinking Skills

FOR SELECTIVE SCHOOL TESTS, OPPORTUNITY CLASS TEST AND PROBLEM SOLVING

Use pencil when filling out this sheet

Fill in the circle correctly			
●	(B)	(C)	(D)

If you make a mistake neatly cross it out and circle the correct response			
⊗	●	(C)	(D)

MULTIPLE CHOICE ANSWER SHEET

1	(A)	(B)	(C)	(D)	21	(A)	(B)	(C)	(D)
2	(A)	(B)	(C)	(D)	22	(A)	(B)	(C)	(D)
3	(A)	(B)	(C)	(D)	23	(A)	(B)	(C)	(D)
4	(A)	(B)	(C)	(D)	24	(A)	(B)	(C)	(D)
5	(A)	(B)	(C)	(D)	25	(A)	(B)	(C)	(D)
6	(A)	(B)	(C)	(D)	26	(A)	(B)	(C)	(D)
7	(A)	(B)	(C)	(D)	27	(A)	(B)	(C)	(D)
8	(A)	(B)	(C)	(D)	28	(A)	(B)	(C)	(D)
9	(A)	(B)	(C)	(D)	29	(A)	(B)	(C)	(D)
10	(A)	(B)	(C)	(D)	30	(A)	(B)	(C)	(D)
11	(A)	(B)	(C)	(D)	31	(A)	(B)	(C)	(D)
12	(A)	(B)	(C)	(D)	32	(A)	(B)	(C)	(D)
13	(A)	(B)	(C)	(D)	33	(A)	(B)	(C)	(D)
14	(A)	(B)	(C)	(D)	34	(A)	(B)	(C)	(D)
15	(A)	(B)	(C)	(D)	35	(A)	(B)	(C)	(D)
16	(A)	(B)	(C)	(D)	36	(A)	(B)	(C)	(D)
17	(A)	(B)	(C)	(D)	37	(A)	(B)	(C)	(D)
18	(A)	(B)	(C)	(D)	38	(A)	(B)	(C)	(D)
19	(A)	(B)	(C)	(D)	39	(A)	(B)	(C)	(D)
20	(A)	(B)	(C)	(D)	40	(A)	(B)	(C)	(D)

Critical Thinking Skills

FOR SELECTIVE SCHOOL TESTS, OPPORTUNITY CLASS TEST AND PROBLEM SOLVING

Use pencil when filling out this sheet

Fill in the circle correctly			
●	B	C	D

If you make a mistake neatly cross it out and circle the correct response			
⊗	●	C	D

MULTIPLE CHOICE ANSWER SHEET

1	A	B	C	D	21	A	B	C	D
2	A	B	C	D	22	A	B	C	D
3	A	B	C	D	23	A	B	C	D
4	A	B	C	D	24	A	B	C	D
5	A	B	C	D	25	A	B	C	D
6	A	B	C	D	26	A	B	C	D
7	A	B	C	D	27	A	B	C	D
8	A	B	C	D	28	A	B	C	D
9	A	B	C	D	29	A	B	C	D
10	A	B	C	D	30	A	B	C	D
11	A	B	C	D	31	A	B	C	D
12	A	B	C	D	32	A	B	C	D
13	A	B	C	D	33	A	B	C	D
14	A	B	C	D	34	A	B	C	D
15	A	B	C	D	35	A	B	C	D
16	A	B	C	D	36	A	B	C	D
17	A	B	C	D	37	A	B	C	D
18	A	B	C	D	38	A	B	C	D
19	A	B	C	D	39	A	B	C	D
20	A	B	C	D	40	A	B	C	D